AquaGuide
Discus

Bernd Degen

CONTENTS

First published in the UK in 2002 by
Interpet Publishing,
Vincent Lane,
Dorking,
Surrey RH4 3YX,
England

English text © 2002 by
Interpet Publishing Ltd.

All rights reserved

ISBN 1-84286-037-2

The recommendations in this book
are given without any guarantees
on the part of the author and
publisher. If in doubt, seek the
advice of a vet or aquatic specialist.

Translation: Heike de Ste. Croix

Originally published in Germany in
1999 by bede-Verlag,
Bühlfelderweg 12,
D-94239 Ruhmannsfelden
© 1999 by bede-Verlag

Picture Credits
Unless otherwise credited in the
captions, all photographs in this
book are the property of bede-
Verlag.
For the supply of pictures, thanks
are due to Fumitoshi Mori, Japan;
Aqualife Taiwan; ADA Takashi
Amano, Japan; Aqualife Japan.

For many aquarists discus are the kings of the freshwater aquarium. Discus live naturally in the River Amazon and its tributaries. At first, after their discovery and later import into Europe, keeping discus was a skill reserved for the specialist only. However, after some years it became possible to breed discus from the original wild stock. This was the beginning of the success story of discus in home aquariums in our country. Gradually discus taken from the wild were replaced in the aquarium by turquoise-coloured offspring which displayed much more vivid colours. In the course of the past 20 years the offspring of all colour varieties became so sought after that constant efforts were made to create new colours.

Discus are sometimes said to be difficult to care for, but anyone who has taken a serious interest in these species will have discovered that keeping and breeding them is quite easy provided that the basic rules of aquarium care and fishkeeping are observed.

There are essentially two types of discus lovers. The first group consists of the many aquarists who buy discus because they like the fish and want to keep them. However, if young discus are kept in an aquarium with other species, some will inevitably be

The Amazon river and its tributaries are important to the people who live next to the water. This is where everyday life takes place.

lost. As a result the frustrated aquarist will eventually give up keeping these fish. But this does not have to happen as long as you observe the basic rules

A typical river bank of the Rio Negro. It is extremely difficult and incredibly hard work to penetrate the jungle.

which this book will teach you. Discus are easy to keep in an aquarium and do not easily succumb to illness. For a discus to die in an aquarium, a lot will have to go wrong.

Are you successful in rearing your discus, in keeping them and perhaps even in breeding them? Then you will

During the rainy season vast areas of the rain forest are flooded and numerous lakes are formed. The water heats up quickly to 30°C (86°F) and thus provides an ideal breeding ground for discus.
Photo: Mori

An underwater view of a slow-flowing river in the Amazon region. The river bed is covered with dead plants.
Photo: Mori

judge keeping discus a very satisfying hobby and one day you will probably find yourself part of the second group of aquarists who devote themselves to these fish. Smitten by discus fever, you can be counted among the aquarists who have successfully bred discus!

Is the discus really a problem fish?

Why is it always said that the discus is a difficult fish? The only possible answer is that many aquarists believe that keeping these fish is a job only for skilled specialists. But the discus is only regarded as a difficult fish because it has been labelled as such. Its reputation for being difficult to keep and breed is a myth that has been per-petuated for many years. On the contrary, incorrect or careless keeping practices are

Discus are happiest in a tank with fine sand and roots; the wood provides them with a screen behind which they can hide.

the only causes for discus to suffer from diseases. Discus are tougher and longer-lived than most other ornamental fish.

The most important element in the correct care of these fish is the water. The water in their natural habitat is extremely soft and it contains many organic substances which are vital for the fish. Discus can be kept easily in an aquarium with medium hard water of 10-15°dH. This level of hardness should be reduced when breeding and this can be achieved with either a reverse osmosis unit, ionic exchange resins or water-softening liquids. The pH value of the water also plays an important part – pH values between 5.5 to 7.0 are considered

ideal for keeping discus. But whatever you do, you must avoid altering the pH value with acids. Even the slightest mistake using acids to soften the water can have fatal consequences for the fish. Small adjustments to the pH value can be made by filtering the water through peat which will reduce the pH value slowly. In order to increase the pH value slightly and to stabilize it, activated carbon makes an ideal filter.

Special attention must be paid to the water's temperature. Discus love warm water, because the water in their natural habitat is always between 29° and 32°C (84° and 90°F). The ideal temperature for the keeping of discus is therefore between 29° and 30°C

(84° and 86°F). Temperatures below 28°C (82°F) are to be avoided at all times, as the fish will begin to feel uncomfortable in these conditions which may lead to the first signs of illness. Changes in water temperature also have a stimulating effect on discus, so a partial water change with the addition of some colder or warmer water can stimulate spawning, provided of course it is done during the spawning season. As it is quite difficult to prevent bacteria attack in a small aquarium containing a relatively small volume of water, it must be emphasized that the best prevention is a partial water change. If your tap water does not have the correct pH value, then it is advisable to filter the water through an activated carbon filter before filling the aquarium.

If the aquarium is generously stocked or if too little water is changed, its nitrate and nitrite levels can rise. These toxic substances can be eliminated either by changing the water or by using a nitrate exchange resin.

Of course feeding also plays an important role in the well-being of discus. Food has to be varied and it makes sense to provide your discus with a balanced diet. If you offer an unbalanced diet, then you should not be surprised to find that the females will not spawn and their colours will fade.

Some aquarists want to keep their discus in a fully equipped aquarium stocked with plants, which is understandable. It is important to be careful with regard to the bottom of the aquarium and any roots you may introduce. The bottom especially can harbour dangers. Food remains can settle and decay in gravel which is too coarse. It is better to keep the floor of the aquarium smooth to prevent unwanted deposits of food remains. It is also important to skim uneaten food off the surface of the water. Some roots can start to rot and the water will give off an unpleasant odour. Ideal water conditions will ensure that nitrate and nitrite levels are kept low and thus prevent many problems with discus care.

Where do discus come from?
The Amazon basin is home to discus which chiefly live in Brazilian waters. However, they are occasionally seen in Peru, Colombia and Venezuela. The gigantic rain forests with their numerous large rivers offer an ideal habitat for many species. Several of the Amazon tributaries rise in the Andes and they can be divided into three types.

They are the so-called whitewater, blackwater and clearwater rivers. The

best-known whitewater rivers are the Amazon, the Rio Solimoes, the Rio Branco and the Rio Madeira. Of the clearwater rivers, the Rio Tapajos and Rio Xingu are the most significant. The Rio Negro is the king of the blackwater rivers and is well-known to many aquarists.

During the rainy season vast areas of the Amazon basin are flooded when the rivers rise by as much as 10 metres (33ft). Strong storms further contribute to wide-scale flooding and numerous lakes are formed which do not exist for long. These temporary lakes provide ideal breeding grounds for the fish. High water temperatures caused by strong sunlight encourage the discus to spawn. At the same time many micro-organisms develop, so-called infusoria, which provide plentiful food for the young fish.

Heavy rainfalls start around January time in the Amazon basin, when the rivers rise slowly and vast areas are flooded. This can last well into June. The water begins to subside slowly in July and the lowest water levels are experienced during October and November. As is it difficult to catch discus during the rainy season, fishermen are confined to the narrower branches of the river systems with their lower water levels. Once the flooding has subsided, the main season for export of wild-caught discus begins which is during our winter months from October to

The rivers of the Amazon region are impressive even during the dry season.

March. However, as the main discus export businesses in Manaus have built vast aquariums, it is now possible for them to sell and export discus

During the rainy season many trees are below water level, which provides good shelter for a variety of ornamental fish and their brood.

outside the normal capture season.

The capture of discus in the wild is difficult and is generally done by native fishermen. Whole families can earn a living from capturing ornamental fish. Catching such fish is an important source of income for the few families who live along the river banks. If they were to lose this income they might instead have to burn down parts of the forest in order to establish banana plantations, for example. So aquatics helps to protect the tropical rain forests and even preserves species.

Discus are either caught in nets, which are set up along the banks and later drawn in, or they are caught by night by boats operating along the river banks. Discus sleep at night when they lie stationary between roots and tree branches in the water at the edges of the river banks or between flooded trees. Once they have been spotted by the fishermen, they can be caught easily with hand nets. However, they don't exactly line up at the river banks waiting to be

Threatening thunderclouds appear regularly during the rainy season followed by tremendous downpours.

trapped! Once caught, they are kept in plastic tubs and transported to the holding tanks – the water is changed several times daily during transit.

Each lorry will carry hundreds of these plastic tubs to the export plants where the fish are transferred to large tanks. They are then categorized before they are offered for sale. Sometimes it can be several months before the fish are exported. It is, therefore, important to acclimatize them quickly and feed them correctly once they arrive in our aquariums.

Hundreds of wild discus are kept in large tiled concrete basins before being exported.

How did the discus get its name?

Discus are members of the cichlid family. Their home is the Amazon basin and its tributaries in South America. This is the only place where discus are found in the wild. The typical round bodyshape, which reminds us of a discus in athletics, gives them their name. At present there is some confusion over the

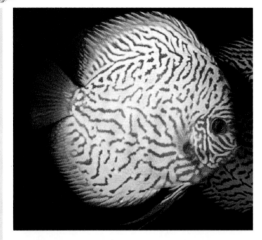

Turquoise discus are widespread among the descendants of wild discus. Photo: Mori

classification of wild discus and there is certainly going to be a reform of the system. There are five wild species categorized by their appearance and colour. These are the classic wild species:

- ***Symphysodon discus discus*** HECKEL, 1840 – Heckel or Real Discus
- ***Symphysodon discus willischwartzii*** BURGESS, 1981 – Blueheaded Discus

The Heckel discus is easily identified by its prominent central stripe. If kept in optimum conditions, the Heckel looks magnificent. Photo: Mori

Crossbreeds can also be found among wild discus, as each discus species can be crossed with another. Such crossbreeds are very popular with aquarists as they are unique.
Photo: Mori

- *Symphysodon aequifasciatus aequifasciatus* PELLEGRIN, 1904 – Green Discus
- *Symphysodon aequifasciatus axelrodi* SCHULTZ, 1960 – Brown Discus
- *Symphysodon aequifasciatus haraldi* SCHULTZ, 1960 – Blue Discus

The **Heckel discus**, first described by Jacob HECKEL in 1840, is the easiest to recognize. This Heckel discus comes from the Rio Negro area and was described as "*Symphysodon discus*". The Heckel discus is easily identified by its nine clearly defined vertical stripes. Discus usually have nine vertical stripes all of equal strength and visibility on their bodies. The Heckel discus is different – its first stripe which runs through the eye, the fifth which runs through the middle of the body, and the ninth stripe at the tail are all particularly distinctive.

This is what distinguishes the Heckel discus from the other discus species. The prominent middle stripe clearly identifies this species.

Heckel discus are somewhat more

A brown wild discus from the Belém area.
Photo: Mori

to 4.5. Heckels are happiest if kept in an aquarium with acidic soft water where they will develop into magnificent strong specimens.

Breeding Heckel discus is very difficult even today and they are therefore classified as the hardest discus to breed. Only very few serious discus lovers have been successful in raising them.

However, all other wild discus are bred in large quantities and are the ancestors of today's highly-bred discus species.

difficult to keep in the aquarium than other discus, as they come from the waters of the Rio Negro and are used to a very low pH value of between 3.2

Not much is known about the

Evenly coloured brown discus were not very popular for a long time, but they are now enjoying a revival.
Photo: Mori

blueheaded discus as it has not been possible to import this species successfully into Europe.

The **brown discus** got its name from the well-known American discus specialist Dr. Herbert R. AXELROD, who collected many brown discus in the area around Belém in Brazil. Many are still caught today in the waters around Santarém and Alenquer and in the Rio Tocantins, the Rio Tapajos and the Rio Xingu. In recent years brown discus have become quite fashionable again because new varieties with an intense red-brown colour have been discovered. The base colour of brown discus varies from light-yellow to dark-brown depending on its origins. The body is covered with nine vertical stripes, the first running through the eye as it does in all other species of discus. If fed well and kept in ideal conditions brown discus will develop a strong rusty brown colour which makes them even more interesting. The edges of the fins and the head are often marked with faint turquoise stripes which gives the brown discus a harmonious appearance.

Blue discus were first introduced into Europe in the 1950s and successfully bred shortly after this. Blue discus are found in the Rio Purus and Manacapuru basin. In most cases the base colour of the front of the body is a browny hue and the back of the body has a strong blue sheen. The body, especially the area around the head and ventral fins, is covered with intense blue stripes which have given the fish its name. Their overall appearance is more colourful and the markings are more distinctive than other discus. If the whole body of the blue discus is covered with blue stripes, then it is called a "royal blue" discus – such specimens are very valuable.

Green discus often come from the Lago Tefé or Rio Tefé. Their base colour is dark brown-green and,

Blue discus whose bodies are covered with blue stripes are described as "royal blue". This is one of the most expensive varieties. Photo: Mori

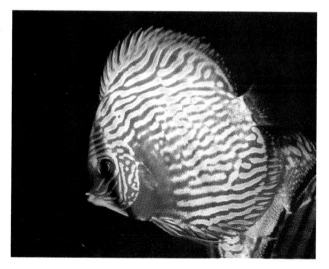

depending on their origin, they may have several turquoise body stripes. Green discus with plentiful red spots on their bellies generally originate from the Tefé region and they are therefore also called Tefé discus. Green discus look quite different from their blue and brown relatives, and the green glimmer of their body colouring can be so vivid that it is quite possible that the later turquoise discus and flat discus were bred from them.

Why are discus so popular?

Discus are the kings of the freshwater aquarium and this explains a lot. But why are they considered to be the kings of the aquarium? Discus are large fish and their bodies can measure up to 20cm (8in) in diameter. This fact alone makes them imposing inhabitants of the aquarium and the focus of attention. Discus are very colourful fish and are available in a wide variety of types. There are always new colour varieties to get enthusiastic about. Discus are also relatively expensive to buy and this is another reason why we give them our special care and attention.

To keep them successfully and perhaps even to breed them presents the aquarist with quite a challenge. Every aquarist eventually reaches the point where he or she wants to deal with difficult species, as it is more challenging than keeping ordinary aquarium fish. There is a sizeable international community interested in keeping discus. During the 1960s people started to breed

Green Tefé discus with plenty of red spots are the absolute favourites among wild discus. Keen breeders are trying to increase the number of spots on the body and to stabilize this characteristic. Photo: Mori

discus are so popular is their remarkable breeding and rearing behaviour. Discus look after their eggs continuously and they are one of the rare breeds of fish that feed their fry with secretions from their own skin. The young fish practically feed on the parents. This strong parent-offspring relationship is really fascinating to observe and makes all the hard work put into breeding them worthwhile.

The American breeder Jack Wattley perfected turquoise blue discus through intensive selective breeding. These solid steel-blue discus are always very popular. Photo: Mori

discus in Europe and the high-quality fish that resulted soon became world-famous.

Many people in southeast Asia are also interested in tropical fish and soon fishkeepers started to breed discus to earn a living. Initially the quality of the discus bred in Asia was very poor, but now they have improved and high-quality discus are reared. Numerous experiments in cross-breeding have produced new colour varieties which constantly amaze us Europeans.

Another fundamental reason why

When bought at eight weeks old, young discus are usually approximately 5cm (2in) in size and not very colourful. However, it gives every aquarist tremendous satisfaction when he or she successfully raises these youngsters into impressive discus measuring between 16cm and 18cm (6.5-7in). This surely is another reason why discus have become so popular.

Caring for your discus

Discus and corydoras can easily be kept in the same tank if it is provided with a sandy substrate, where they forage for food.

The right aquarium

Whatever aquarium you choose for discus, it can never be too big; on the contrary it is usually too small. Discus are large fish and they should be kept in relatively large communities as this makes them feel more comfortable. Therefore the aquarium should be at least 100cm (40in) long. Naturally, if you have the space, it would be better to install a still larger aquarium. The height and the depth of the aquarium must not be less than 50cm (20in); this is really the minimum size for a discus aquarium. An aquarium 120cm (48in) in length and 60cm (24in) in depth

and height is ideal in which to keep eight to ten discus comfortably. Particularly when raising discus it is a good idea to keep a group of at least

eight fish, but 12 to 15 is better still.
Whether discus should be kept in an aquarium with aquatic plants is often a controversial issue. Many

The combination of discus and aquatic plants can be a harmonious one as this picture shows, where discus are kept with angelfish and tetras. Provided that the water conditions are right and sufficient carbon dioxide is available, both fish and plants will thrive.
Photo: Kilian

discus breeders would not recommend keeping discus and plants together as the fish can succumb to diseases more easily. But this does not have to be the case if certain basic rules are observed. With good preparation and by observing correct techniques, an aquarium containing

plants can be looked after easily for at least five to six years without the need to empty and restock it.

What plants can be introduced into a discus aquarium?

Aquatic plants need nutritious soil. However, this is not necessarily ideal for discus as this type of soil produces substances which can cause complications for the fish. The soil, however, is needed to encourage plant growth and it may become necessary to add some granulated nutrients into the substrate. Installation of a thermostatically

controlled cable heating system can also be beneficial to the plants. This is installed on the floor of the aquarium to keep the plants warm. It encourages a gentle circulation of water through the soil which

transports nutrients to the plant roots.

When installing this type of heating, it should ideally be covered with approximately 5cm (2in) of gravel with a grain of 1-2mm (0.04-0.08in). This grain size provides an ideal circulation through the biological filters which break down nitrates can be installed in such an aquarium. However, if the plants are healthy, they will use nitrates themselves as a nutrient and thus provide good water conditions. But aquatic plants also need carbon dioxide to develop properly. For this

To create a functional discus community it is essential that all fish undergo a quarantine period. Any plants introduced to an aquarium must be able to tolerate temperatures of 28°-30°C (82°-86°F).

substrate. Aquatic plants prefer slight water movement and gentle filtration, conditions that also suit discus. You should therefore choose a filter system which does not cause undue water turbulence. Long-term reason ready-made fertilizers containing carbon dioxide are available which convert carbon dioxide into carbonic acid. The pH-value can be reduced slightly with this carbon dioxide fertilizer, which

is beneficial to the discus as they prefer slightly acid pH values of between 5.0 to 7.0.

Which plants are best suited to a discus aquarium?

Discus love a water temperature of at least 28°C (82°F) and so it is important to choose the plants which also tolerate such high temperatures.

All *Echinodorus* Amazon sword plants are suitable, and they come in all shapes and sizes. Very small species are ideally suited to planting in the front of the aquarium. The larger types of *Echinodorus* can be planted individually or used as a background plant. Apart from the *Echinodorus* species, cryptos are also suitable as they thrive in high water temperatures. Their origin does not make them perfect for an Amazon aquarium but not everything has to be perfect. *Cryptocoryne* species grow very slowly. *Aponogetons* are also suitable for a discus aquarium. After a few months they become dormant for a period of time. Once the leaves begin to die down, the tubers can be removed from the aquarium and stored for two months in moist peat in a dark place. After this period of dormancy, the tubers can be reintroduced to the aquarium and soon magnificent leaves will be begin to shoot.

Vallisneria species are lovely plants for the discus aquarium, especially the large twisted vallis which is very decorative. Vallis also makes a very pretty background plant.

All these varieties provide numerous possible combinations of aquatic plants so your planting ideas are almost unlimited. It is best not to have too many plants initially as the natural instinct of discus is to hide in the jungle of plants. This concealment behaviour is perfectly normal. Regular care will allow the discus to get accustomed to you until they recognize you and appear at the surface at feeding time.

An aquarium containing plants has to have the appropriate lighting. It is fairly simple to find the correct lighting for a discus aquarium that also houses plants – fluorescent tubes have proved to be suitable. It is often claimed that discus need only subdued lighting as too bright a light will frighten them, but this is not always the case. Their natural habitat includes the sunny rivers of the Amazon basin which enjoy plenty of natural daylight. Naturally, visibility in these rivers is different from that in an aquarium and the fish also have a larger area into which to retreat when they need to escape. An aquarium with limited space offers little room for such escape strategies and the

discus have to hide behind plants and other furnishings. Discus quickly get used to movement in front of the aquarium and soon lose their initial fear. However, this only applies if the discus are healthy. Position the aquarium in such a way that the shadow of an onlooker is not directly cast onto it which might otherwise trigger a flight reaction. Always avoid placing an aquarium next to a window or a door. Both for the fish and the observer it is good to position the lower edge of the aquarium at a height of approximately 80cm (30in) which means that the fish swim at eye level when you are sitting in front of the aquarium. Fluorescent tubes are available in different colours and each aquarist can choose his favourite lighting. Fluorescent tubes which emit a large proportion of red light are very popular with discus lovers as they emphasize the beautiful red colours of the discus. Special plant lights are also available which are recommended for densely planted aquariums. Natural daylight and these spectrally enhanced tubes are a perfect combination.

Aquariums stocked with plants should ideally not be taller than 60cm (24in) to guarantee good plant growth. If the water is deeper than 60cm (24in), not enough light can get to the lower-lying plants. Just as

in nature, an aquarium should be lit daily for approximately 12 hours. Use a time clock to regulate your aquarium lighting. The lighting period can be extended to 14 hours if required.

Substrates and furnishings

Discus are mainly bred in aquariums without any decorations. A simple clay urn may be added where the discus will lay their eggs. Breeders want to keep it as simple as possible and maintain a hygienic aquarium to ensure that they lose as few young fish

Peaceful catfish and discus can be kept in the same tank. However, once discus start to spawn the catfish might attack the fry.

as possible. However, such sterile aquariums are not very attractive for keeping discus in the home. It is only right that the majestic discus are kept in an appropriately beautifully equipped aquarium.

Fine sand typically forms the bottom in the discus' natural habitat. Their round body shape makes it more difficult for discus to pick up food from the bottom than it is for fish with elongated mouths. They use a technique whereby they blow into the sand to stir up food which then floats a few centimetres above the bottom where it is easy to pick up. Fine sand therefore makes a perfect base for a discus aquarium provided the layer is not too thick. Fine coral sand in layers of 1-2cm (0.4-0.8in) is also the preferred substrate in marine aquariums. Such a thin layer is easily maintained and quickly cleaned. If aquatic gravel is used as a base, it should not be too coarse. The grain should not be larger than 2-3mm (0.08-0.1in). If coarser grain gravel is used, food particles will settle into it and later decay.

Each type of soil must be cleaned under running water before spreading it on the aquarium floor. If you wish to introduce plants, then the soil must be spread slighter thicker in the appropriate places so that the plants can root in it. It is also possible to place individual plants in clay pots on the aquarium floor. This is a good compromise if you want to keep the aquarium free of any soil. Another alternative is to divide the aquarium floor into two zones. The back half can have a thicker layer of soil kept in place with either stones or a strip of glass providing sufficient depth for plants to root. The other half of the aquarium can be soil-free or covered with just a thin layer of sand just 1cm (0.4in) in depth. This provides a suitable feeding ground for the fish and any food remains can easily be picked off the floor. Just a little imagination is needed to create such a terraced aquarium which is also easy to maintain.

As discus live in soft water, only introduce furnishings or decorations into the aquarium that will not give off any substances that may harden the water.

Some aquarists also like to introduce wood or roots into a discus aquarium which give the impression of the discus' natural habitat. In their home waters discus live among tree roots and under the branches of trees that have been flooded. When buying wood you must ensure that it is of a suitable variety for long-term siting in an aquarium. Wood must not rot or give off a noxious gas or harmful substances. Introducing the wrong wood into the discus aquarium has often been the reason for sick discus. You should consult an expert in a specialist shop.

The background of the aquarium has to be designed appropriately to

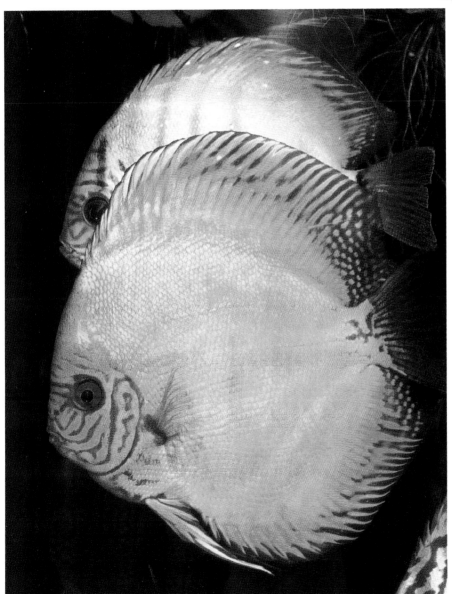

Cobalt-blue discus with bright red eyes are absolute highlights of selective discus breeding. 28°C (82°F) is the minimum temperature for discus to feel comfort- able. Only then will they begin to develop their magnificent colours. Photo: Mori

make it look attractive. Discus also enjoy an enclosed swimming space and a decorative back panel gives them some "psychological" security. The design for such a back panel can be varied. One simple idea is to paint the exterior back wall. But don't choose dark colours as they take away a lot of light and make the aquarium look smaller. Go for mid-blue, green and mid-brown. The back and side panels of the aquarium can also be covered either with a plastic film or foil printed with plant designs which is available from specialist outlets. Another alternative is to place painted polystyrene against the back wall which also acts as insulation. Made-to-measure synthetic back panels are also available which can be directly fixed to the back wall of the aquarium. Some of these landscapes look quite fantastic and make the aquarium look really wonderful. Unfortunately, they are expensive.

Heating your aquarium

While it is ideal to heat a discus aquarium which contains plants rooted in gravel with a cable heater in order to keep the roots of the plants warm, thermostatically controlled immersion heating elements are the conventional form of heating for a discus aquarium. Cable heaters should also ideally be controlled by a thermostat to avoid an unwanted rise in the water's temperature. Often undergravel heating is not sufficient and thermostatically controlled immersion heaters have to be added; they are available in different wattages which makes it easy to select the right size. If your aquarium is situated in a heated room, the rule of thumb to follow is one watt per two to three litres of aquarium water. The advantage of thermostatically controlled heating is that the desired water temperature can be set on the heater and the water kept at a constant temperature.

During the spawning season a variation in temperature can be of benefit to the discus and the water temperature can be raised slowly to 32°C (90°F) with a thermostatic heater to encourage the discus to spawn. The temperature can just as easily lowered by the same method. The heater is usually fitted directly into the aquarium, but on aquariums with large exterior filters it can be installed in the filter canister. If it is installed in the canister, the water must flow constantly around the heating element to avoid it overheating. Before you carry out any work on the aquarium you must always disconnect all electric appliances to avoid accidents. Usually these appliances are fitted with a safety switch. You can buy a special safety switch for larger aquariums which is directly connected to the electrical circuit which provides the power to the aquarium. You must always read the safety instructions.

The ideal temperature for keeping discus is on average 29°C (84°F). Only when the water has reached this temperature do the discus really feel at home. If kept at lower temperatures of 25° or 26°C (77°-79°F) discus begin to feel uncomfortable and tend to become prone to diseases.

Many discus breeders swear by raising the water temperature as the first treatment for ailing discus. However, a rise in temperature up to 36°C (97°F) can sometimes be

harmful and beginners should avoid using this treatment. It is important to carry out any changes in water temperature gradually. For example, a rise in temperature from 29°C (84°F) to 33°C (91°F) should be carried out over a period of 24 hours so that the fish gradually become accustomed to these temperature changes. Similarly a reduction in the temperature should be performed over the same length of time. If your discus are receiving medication, the water temperature should not be too high and with some medication e.g. Masoten (Bayer) the water temperature should even be lowered to 26°C (79°F) while treating your discus.

As you can see, water temperature plays a vital role in the well-being of your discus.

Discus in the aquarium

As this picture of a cobalt blue discus shows, there is nothing more beautiful for the aquarist than a nicely planted discus aquarium. Photo: ADA Amano

These kings of the aquarium are best displayed in a well set-up show-tank where they will capture the attention of any admirer. The combination of dark wood and fresh green plants makes a magnificent picture and the varieties of discus provide a colourful contrast. Small discus are not really suitable for such an aquarium as they are still growing and their feeding has to be controlled, which is quite difficult in a large show-tank where the fish can easily hide.

Before you plant your chosen plants into the aquarium you must provide a layer of sand at least 4cm (1.6in) deep. The sand should neither be too fine nor too coarse.

Although keeping these lovely species in an aquarium stocked with plants is still the exception rather than the rule, discus do come into contact with aquatic plants in flooded areas in their natural habitat. It is a good idea not to overstock the tank with plants to begin with, as this provides numerous hiding places for the discus. Without dense plant growth they will acclimatize better, so that later, when the plants are established, they will not be shy to appear in the open. Discus are mostly kept in sterile aquariums for breeding purposes. However, for general display it is more enjoyable to keep discus in tanks such as the one illustrated overleaf. It is also quite possible to breed discus in this type of tank; however, a sterile aquarium is much better suited for breeding purposes.

When installing a tank for discus, it is important to provide sufficient swimming space as the fish otherwise tend to hide. This swimming space should of course be established at the front of the aquarium. Large pieces of wood are situated at either side which not only look pretty but are also useful. Naturally, the wood must be thoroughly cleaned and watered before positioning. A specialist shop will offer a variety of beautiful roots and pieces of wood which are suitable for aquariums. Mopani wood is ideal as it is very heavy and quickly sinks to the bottom. You must never use rotting wood as it gives off toxic substances.

Rosette plants are good for deep discus aquariums as they do not need a lot of light. Easy-to-grow plants which can withstand high water temperatures are generally preferred for discus tanks.

The tall water plants which you can see in the picture emphasize the colour of the bogwood while the small rosette plants in the foreground emphasize the size of the wood. Healthy plant growth in a discus aquarium is important as the plants absorb large amounts of harmful

It is a good idea to draw up a plan of your planting scheme before stocking a large discus aquarium. Photo: Aqualife Japan

substances from the water. Healthy plants contribute to good water conditions for the fish. If growth is restricted, then this can have a negative effect on the fish. If wilted leaves are allowed to rot, the level of harmful substances in the water will rise and may harm the discus.

The picture below shows a large aquarium, 180 x 60 x 60cm (70 x 24 x 24in) in size, but a similar underwater aquascape can also be created in a smaller tank.

The floor is covered with washed sand and as the tank is only partially planted up, it is important not to add any plant fertilizer in the unplanted areas. Use plant fertilizer carefully and only in places where large plants are to be placed. It must be stressed that wood and roots produce acidic tannins which will affect the water's acidity. It is therefore sensible to test the water regularly for acidity, nitrate and nitrite content. Suitable water testers are available from any specialist shop. It might also be beneficial to rinse the wood several days prior to using these testers.

Also smell the water in your aquarium occasionally to check if the wood gives off a musty smell. If discus

1 *Heteranthera zosteraefolia*
2 *Bacopa monnieri*
3 *Aponogeton ulvaceus*
4 *Echinodorus osiris*

5 *Echinodorus amazonicus*
6 *Echinodorus quadricostatus*
7 *Vallisneria spiralis*
8 *Mayaca vandellii*

are not well, their colours darken, which is often a result of rotting wood.

An aquarium should be fitted with an appropriate filter, but it is important that the waste water does not flow out through the filter too quickly as this would disturb the discus. Discus do not like strong currents and this also applies to water plants. It is advisable to feed the filtered water into the tank via a diffuser pipe with several small holes.

When installing lighting you must ensure that the small plants get sufficient light. This is not a problem in tanks that are 60cm (24in) in height or more. A carbon dioxide fertilizer

Peaceful fellow tank-dwellers, mainly from the Amazon region, can be kept with discus. Lovely catfish are ideal to add colour to a discus aquarium. Angelfish also make good companions for discus, although they are greedy eaters. Angelfish and corydoras give the finishing touch to a beautiful show tank.

Which fish can you keep with discus?

will provide sufficient food for the plants which is important as plants thrive on this type of fertilizer. Incidentally, discus are not affected by carbon dioxide fertilizers. Discus are easy to care for in any aquarium with normal lighting and it is wrong to say that discus need subdued light. For the right plant selection look at the drawing on page 29 which gives you the names of the plants and shows where to place them. If you cannot buy the exact plants shown, similar species are available which offer the same potential for a beautiful aquarium.

The background of the example aquarium pictured on pages 28-29 is planted with *Vallisneria spiralis* and *Heteranthera zosterifolia* which make a nice combination with the wood. *Echinodorus amazonicus* and *Echinodorus quadricostatus* have been planted at the front. In their natural habitat discus tend to live near riverbanks covered with plants and overhanging tree roots or under the submerged leaves of the trees. *Mayaca vandellii* is one of the larger plants with delicate leaves. It has a fresh appearance and is easy to keep in high water temperatures. Regular changes of water are beneficial for fish and plants. Only plants with long stalks need to be trimmed and then only once they grow along the surface

of the water. If plants change colour or begin to wilt, introduce some soil fertilizer. However, this should not be necessary provided you use sufficient carbon dioxide fertilizer.

To find the right discus for such an aquarium may require some shopping around. As mentioned previously, avoid introducing smaller discus into this type of tank, and, as discus live in shoals, it is advisable to keep five to ten discus in the tank. They should be at least six months old and approximately 10cm (4in) long. Better still, buy fully grown discus. Before introducing them to your aquarium, they should undergo a quarantine period. Healthy fish have a light colouring and eat well. They should also not be easily startled. Discus are available in various colours and your choice in this respect depends on personal preference and on how much money you wish to spend on your aquarium.

The water
Ideal water for keeping discus is found in only a very few places, as the water companies are trying to increase the pH value of tap water to at least 7.0, or higher. Very acidic water can lead to corrosion of the water pipes. In order to increase the pH value of mains water, mineral salts are added and the water has very high

Discus in the aquarium

Aquarium data

Water temperature:	28°C (82°F)
Tank size:	180 x 60 x 60cm (70 x 24 x 24in)
Lighting:	2 x 30 watt bulbs, pearl white 2 x 30 watt bulbs Grolux or similar, daily lighting duration 12 hours, no natural daylight
Soil:	Riversand or fine dark gravel
Filter:	Exterior filter with bio-chamber
Change of water:	Twice weekly, up to a quarter of the tank contents
Heating:	2 x 200 watt heaters
Fertilizer:	Only a light plant fertilizer because of the discus. Carbon dioxide added at regular intervals.
Water chemistry:	pH value: 6.2, hardness: 1°KH, 3°dH, CO_2 solution content: 10mg/l

electrical conductivity, which is totally unsuitable for rearing discus. Although tap water can be used in a discus tank, the careful aquarist will always run the water over activated carbon before filling the tank. This is best done in a separate water container to which the carbon filter is connected.

Discus can still spawn in water with a pH value of 7 and higher, but very often problems develop quickly with the eggs. It is for this reason that many discus lovers choose to prepare the water before filling the tank. It is not much of a problem to lower the pH value; using a peat filter is one simple way of achieving this. For this you need aquatic peat, which you can buy in any specialist shop, and you fill your filter with it.

To soften aquarium water two standard methods can be used. The simple way to remove salts from the

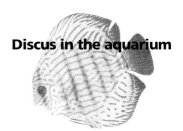

water is with a reverse osmosis unit. You can now buy this equipment in any specialist shop; they are reasonably priced and very useful for the aquarist. Although the amount of water they can process is limited, it is enough to fill several tanks. Reverse osmosis for simple aquatic purposes works with water pressure. The cartridge of this device is attached to the water pipe. Often a additional filter is positioned ahead of the unit to prevent any dirt damaging the membrane. The main part of reverse osmosis unit is a semi-permeable membrane which acts like a sieve and stops salts and other substances from the water filtering through. The high pressure of tap water pushes the clean water through the membrane and the dissolved substances and salts stay in the remaining liquid. Just think of this process as an ultra-fine filter system. As the membrane can be sensitive to chlorine and dirt, it is advisable to position an activated carbon filter ahead of the membrane. The equipment comes complete with this filter.

The filtered water will only contain very few dissolved substances and is similar in composition to distilled water. Distilled water, however, can be lethal to fish and so it is not suitable for using in a tank on its own. You either have to mix this water with normal tap water or use it when changing some of the water of the tank. As the electric conductivity of this water is very low, it can change the pH value which should be constantly monitored in tanks which contain very soft water. This can be done by using simple chemically treated litmus paper or cheap but reliable pH meters. It is important to stabilize the pH value of the water in any aquarium and especially so if you rearing young fish as they react strongly to pH fluctuation which can affect their growth.

The second standard method of softening the water in your tank is by ionic exchange where the water is partially or completely softened with the help of ionic exchange resins. You can test the hardness of the water in your tank with test kits, either using liquid reagents or conductivity meters. Very soft water has a conductivity of $150\mu S/cm$. If you measure a value of between $150\mu S/cm$ and $300\mu S/cm$, then the water is still relatively soft and your discus will feel quite comfortable and you could even breed them in this water. If the electric conductivity rises above $300\mu S/cm$, then the water is harder and any values above $600\mu S/cm$ indicate very hard water which is completely unsuitable for breeding discus. If it is carbon hardness (i.e.

It is possible to breed discus in a fully stocked tank although rearing the fry can be quite difficult as other occupants of the tank will regard them as food.
Photo: ADA Amano

chalk), then partial softening with the aid of a cation exchanger is recommended. If you want to soften your water completely, you have to combine a cation exchanger with an anion exchanger. These are plastic columns filled with small resin balls which are chemically charged. The tap water and tank water are pumped through these columns and the chemical reaction alters the water. Specialist literature on discus is available to tell you which salts to use and in what quantities to use them. Alternatively, any specialist shop which sells the exchange resins and associated kit will be able to give you further advice. Unfortunately, the resins have to be recharged once used, which is quite labour-intensive and has to be carried out with great care as you are handling salt solutions and acids. With the help of ionic exchange kits and reverse osmosis units you will be able to provide the right water for rearing your discus.

Filters

Filters play an important part in the hygiene of your aquarium. It is impossible to keep a well-stocked discus aquarium without a good filtration system and the available options vary depending on whether your tank is set up for keeping or breeding discus. Bacteria in the filter

substrate are the main requirement for the proper functioning of any long-term biological filtration system. The bacteria in the filter substrate cleanse the water and break down any harmful substances which may be present. So you must be careful when cleaning your filtration system not to remove all the filter substrate. This would eliminate all the beneficial bacteria from your tank and the new filter material would not be able to purify the water during the first weeks of operation. Any filter material should be cleaned with lukewarm water which will not destroy any of the bacteria present.

It is also advisable to use a pre-filter with any filtration system. This pre-filter can trap any coarse dirt so that only microscopically small particles will be drawn through to the main filtration system where they are broken down by the action of bacteria.

Complete filtration systems for individual aquariums are available from any specialist shop. There are two types: slow- and fast-acting filters. The fast-acting filter cleans the tank quickly of all the coarse waste matter; however they are not suitable for purifying the water biologically with bacteria – for this purpose you need the slow-acting filter. Depending on the size of the tank, smaller internal

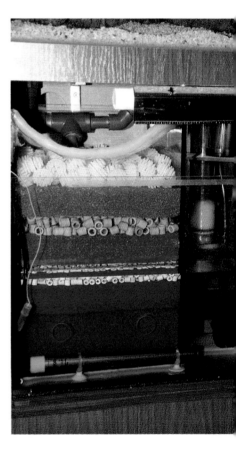

This is a picture of a trickle filter, which discus aquarists build underneath their tanks as they are very long-lasting. However, it is important to use a pre-filter, which can trap any coarse dirt, and to carry out partial water changes on a regular basis. At least 20 per cent of the water in the tank should be changed.

or external filters can be fitted to the sides of the aquarium. For larger tanks canister filters are more appropriate as they can be hidden from view in the cupboard below the tank.

Because of the discus' normal swimming pattern, it is advisable to fit a slow-running filtration system, as the fish do not feel comfortable in fast-flowing water. When choosing a filtration system for a breeding tank, ensure that it does not allow the young fry to be sucked into the filter. The pipes of any such filter can temporarily be covered with protective guards or foam-filled cartridges. Some breeders who own large breeding tanks often connect several tanks to one filtration cycle. Such a community filtration system has advantages as well as dis-advantages. The advantage is that it is easier to keep the correct biological balance in the larger quantity of water. A considerable disadvantage, however, is that any disease will spread to every tank. Individual breeding tanks can be kept clean easily with an air-lift filter.

This has the advantage of operating as a slow-running water filter which can break down nitrates with the help of bacteria in the sponge. Once these filters have been working for a few days, they achieve great results. To clean them, simply rinse the filter briefly in lukewarm water after which it will operate again effectively. A considerable advantage of this filtration system is that young fish cannot be sucked into it.

Correct feeding regimes
Discus are omnivores and their favourite food in Amazon waters are

diet. Mosquito larvae are the classic food for partially grown and adult discus and they are available frozen from all specialist shops. Live mosquito larvae are a bit more difficult to get hold of, but it is quite fascinating from time to time to watch discus devour the live larvae. Apart from the well-known red mosquito larvae, white and black mosquito larvae are also available from your aquatic shop. Unfortunately, red mosquito larvae are not as nutritious as their black and white relatives.

Another problem is that mosquito larvae often can be affected by pollution and so the possibility of the feed being contaminated by heavy metals sometimes present in mosquito larvae should not be ignored. Apart from mosquito larvae, discus

Slow-acting filters are preferable for breeding tanks. It is important that the young discus fry cannot be sucked into the filtration system. Strong water movements should also be avoided during the first days of breeding.

freshwater shrimps, but they also like fruit and seeds which fall into the water during the flooding season. Of course, all mosquito larvae are an absolute delicacy for discus. In captivity discus can be fed on almost any commercially prepared foods. However, it takes time and patience to get the fish accustomed to the new breeders also feed their fish on ready-frozen mixtures of beef and turkey hearts. The more delicate turkey hearts are usually preferred. The disadvantage of feeding these mixes is that they make the water cloudy and so it is essential to remove any uneaten food from the water the same day. Some discus lovers even

prepare their own food mix which can then be frozen in individual servings.

Enchytraeid worms are another valuable live food. It can be quite work-intensive to breed these whiteworms as they are reared in boxes underground. Starter kits for rearing them are available in aquatic shops. To begin with, place the kit in a polystyrene box filled with fine soil. Enchytraeids can be bred easily in a cool cellar. These small worms need to be fed regularly with either white bread soaked in water, oatmeal, rusk or similar foods. The food can also be enriched with vitamins which in turn pass through to the discus. *Artemia* are also a good food for discus. These marine brine shrimps, approximately 8mm (0.03in) long, are quickly devoured by the discus. They make a nutritious feed as their shells contain chitin and they are rich in carotenoids. These carotenoids give the discus their intense colours and, when fed regularly on these crustaceans, it is even possible to intensify the red colours of the fish.

Discus can also be fed on dried food in the form of flakes or granules. Discus pellets are the latest modern feed to be

Provided you give them the appropriate attention, you can get your discus used to almost any type of feed. Special discus granulates make feeding considerably easier.

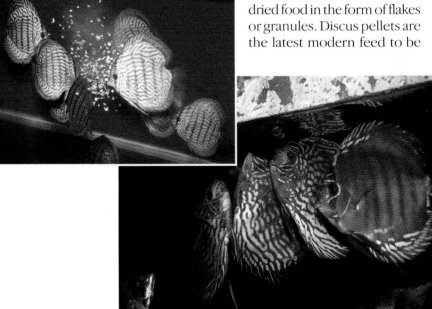

Young fish especially can get used to many types of diet. Here they devour food in tablet form which gives the owner the added advantage of being able to add extra vitamin drops by simply putting them on the tablets before feeding time.

marketed. Leading manufacturers sell these granulated foods, which the discus eat happily once they are used to them.

Granulated food provides a good nutritional basis for the fish and it can be supplemented with enchytraeid worms, mosquito larvae or brine shrimp.

Young discus quickly grow accustomed to a new type of food, but it takes a bit more patience to get older fish used to a new diet. However, you are wrong to expect your discus to feed happily on dried foods thrown into the tank once a day. If at least one fish in the tank is feeding on the new food, it is then quite easy

to get the others accustomed to the new diet.

A day's diet for adult discus should consist of three servings, one serving of a granulate, one serving of whiteworm or mosquito larvae, and finally one serving of brine shrimps. This way the discus get a balanced diet and they will not suffer any nutritional deficiencies. It is not necessary to feed adult discus more often than this. However, this does not apply to young discus, as you want them to grow quickly and not suffer any growth impairment during the formative stages. Regular feeding is necessary and the old saying "feed little but often" applies here. Young discus can be fed up to six or eight times a day, but make sure that you keep the servings small so that all the food is eaten by the young fish within minutes. Because of the increased frequency of feeding, it is essential to carry out regular partial changes of the water in the tank.

It is often said that discus are prone to diseases. But why should a discus succumb to sickness more readily than any other ornamental fish?

It would be difficult to prove this claim in the wild as the conditions in their natural habitat are quite different from those in the aquarium. The risk of infection is higher in the aquarium because of the relatively small amount of water present. Incorrect keeping is the main cause of many diseases. Discus are large fish and they require considerably more water and living space than other ornamental fish. Their imposing appearance and high market value make discus more interesting than smaller and less expensive fish. As a consequence, the owner will quickly notice if something is wrong with his discus, whereas he would perhaps take less notice of smaller fish. The best way to keep your discus healthy is by prevention rather than cure, and this means maintaining good water quality in your tank.

Discus live in slightly acidic water, a factor that has to be taken into account when setting up a discus tank in order to guarantee the health of your fish. The water should have a permanent pH value of between 5.5 and 7.0. Slow increases and decreases in pH value are harmless to the discus provided they do not reach extreme values, especially high ones. Discus lovers sometimes tend to use too many medications. It is thoughtless to do this without coming to the right diagnosis first – you could be harming your fish more than you are doing good. A comprehensive book by Dieter Untergasser, *Discus Health: Selection, Care, Diet, Diseases and Treatments for Discus, Angelfish and Other Cichlids*, explains even the most complicated treatments.

Quite a lot of medicines which are used for treating discus are only available on prescription as they are either used in human or veterinary medicine. If necessary, consult a vet for a diagnosis and to obtain the right medicine.

Ammonia or nitrite poisoning, sudden changes in pH value, temperature variations, lack of oxygen, and environmental toxicity are all disease-causing factors in ornamental fish. Unsuitable transport of the fish, changes in the water environment, overcrowding in the tank and the introduction of diseases by new fish are other likely causes.

The last factor especially is often overlooked and new diseases are consequently brought into the tank because insufficient quarantine times are observed. Always plan your quarantine period before buying new discus.

For this purpose you need to set up a quarantine tank which only contains a single flowerpot, which can serve as a hiding place for the fish. Quarantine should last for at least four weeks during which time you will be able to discover whether your newly acquired discus are ill or healthy. Preventive measures can also be carried out in the quarantine aquarium. The tank should be equipped with a simple sponge filter and heated to 30°C (86°F).

One preventive treatment for discus that does not involve chemicals is warm-water treatment. This is easily carried out in the quarantine tank. The upper limit for this heat treatment is 36°C (97°F). To start with, get yourself a reliable thermometer to monitor the water temperature. Then warm the tank so that the water reaches a temperature of between 30° and 36°C (86°-97°F) during the course of a day. Don't maintain this temperature for longer than three days, however. Then lower the

Emaciated and sick discus have the typical "knife-back" and the eyes seem far too large in relation to the body.

temperature slowly again to 30°C (86°F). This temperature increases the discus' oxygen requirement and their basal metabolism. In addition it is beneficial to hang an airstone in the tank. During the heat treatment the quarantine tank has to be free of chemicals or medicines as their presence would otherwise affect the treatment. It is also likely that

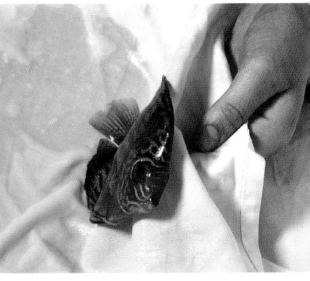

the fish will not feed properly in these temperatures and so it is advisable only to give them as much as they will actually eat at one time. Any uneaten food has to be siphoned off immediately as it would

decay quickly in the warm water.

Unfortunately, all too often aquarists pay too little attention to quarantine and if newly acquired fish seem to look healthy, they are swiftly introduced to an established tank that is already stocked with other fish. This can quickly lead to outbreaks of sickness. Often it is the so-called "discus disease" which is usually transmitted by apparently healthy looking fish. Much has been written about this "discus disease" and by now a variety of treatments are recommended. It is baffling that this disease is transmitted by healthy looking fish. It is quite possible to infect your whole tank stock in virtually no time by introducing newcomers. The newly afflicted fish quickly begin to react to the disease and start to excrete excessive amounts of slime through their mucous membranes. The fish then suddenly turn black and become anxious. Quite often the disease is concealed by a secondary infection which must be tackled first. If the disease is not treated, then the fish will succumb and die within hours or a few days at most. Untergasser describes the precise course of the disease and its treatment in his book *Discus Health: Selection, Care, Diet, Diseases and Treatments for Discus, Angelfish and Other Cichlids*.

The treatment itself is carried out in temperatures between 27° to 28°C (81°-82°F) and the prescribed medication is Nitrofurantoin and Neomycin. Both medicines are only available on prescription from a vet. You must therefore explain your situation to the vet so that you can obtain the 100mg Nitrofurantoin (Ratiopharm retard) capsules from him. Neomycin is available as soluble neomycinsulphate also on prescription. Dissolve 2g (0.07oz) of neomycinsulphate per 100 litres (22gal) of water in a glass of lukewarm water. Add one 100mg (3.5oz) capsule of Nitrofurantoin per 40 litres (9gal) of water. Then pour this mixture into the tank containing the sick fish. A visible improvement should be noticeable in the discus on the second day. Ensure that the tank is thoroughly aerated. Always consult your vet when using such treatments.

The biofilter may have to be disconnected from the tank, cleaned and reconnected as they tend to tip up or get blocked with mucus during the treatment. Should the quality of the water deteriorate during treatment, then you must carry out a partial water change and, depending on the amount of water replaced, add an appropriate amount of the recommended medication.

The treatment is completed after

An attack of "discus disease" will cause the fish to be covered in a grey coating and it will start to shed large amounts of body slime, which can quickly lead to death.

five days and it is now important to look after the water carefully. However, you have to remember that the recovered fish can still pass on the disease to the remaining stock. It can take up to several months before the fish have fully recovered and are no longer carriers of the disease.

The most common illness discus suffer from is weight loss. A darkening of their colours and loss of appetite are the first symptoms. If your discus start to isolate themselves and stop eating, alarm bells should ring as this could mean that they are suffering from a flagellate attack. For years

metronidazole has been used by aquarists to treat flagellates. Metronidazole is only available on prescription though so you will have to contact your vet. The human medicine "Clont" (Bayer) is the best know medication. Pure metronidazole can also be obtained from the chemist. One tablet of "Clont" contains 250mg (9oz) of metronidazole and one tablet should be added to 50 litres (11gal) of aquarium water. This medication should stay for four days in the tank after which you must carry out a partial water change so that the medication is removed

from the water through an activated carbon filter. Unfortunately, many flagellates have already gained immunity against many medicines and so it is recommended that you repeat the treatment after a week. If your discus are still eating when they exhibit the first symptoms of the disease, you can mix some metronidazole into their food. This can be more or less difficult depending on the type of food you use. If you feed your discus on turkey- or beefheart-mix, then simply mix 100g (3.5oz) of feed with 250mg (9oz) of metronidazole. You must however dissolve the powder in 2-3 table-spoonsful of hot water before adding it to the food. If your discus prefer food tablets, simply mix 250mg (9oz) of metronidazole powder with six finely crushed tablets and add a few drops of water to make it into a thick dough which is then spread evenly onto ten other food tablets and left to dry overnight. You can then treat your discus with metronidazole the next morning with the prepared food tablets. Your fish should be given this preparation for four to five days; if they eat it, they should recover quickly. Their colours will brighten, the fish will become more active and enjoy their food again. A repeat treatment is however recommended which should start two weeks after

the first treatment has been concluded.

Another problem with caring for discus is gill flukes, which are quite common and usually transmitted by newly introduced fish. "Masoten" is the best-known medication amongst discus lovers. It contains Metrifonat (Trichlorophon) and is mostly used in ponds. It has very strong side effects if the wrong dosage is used in an aquarium or if the water temperature exceeds 28°C (82°F) during the treatment. In any case a treatment with Masoten will put your discus under strain. Before treating your discus for gill flukes you should also be sure that it is the right diagnosis. Untergasser describes the diagnosis and treatments of this disease in his books. A second well-known medicine is "Flubenol 5%" which contains five per cent flubendazole. Flubenol treatment is no longer such a controversial treatment, but some reports indicate that discus repeatedly treated with Flubenol may start to swim with their heads down and have to be put down. Therefore, prevention is always the better option; this way you can fight the cause of any possible disease in its initial stages.

Masoten is also used as a long-term bath for the treatment of gill flukes. 50mg (1.75oz) of Masoten should be

used per 100 litres (22gal) of water. The treatment lasts for four days. It is vital that the water temperature is reduced to below 28°C (82°F). It is also beneficial to replace a quarter of the water and add a corresponding dose of Masoten daily during the four-day treatment. Once the treatment is completed, carry out a partial water change and remove the medication with an activated carbon filter.

Also take great care when treating your fish with Masoten as it can be lethal to other species, especially catfish and salmon.

As mentioned, the medication Flubenol 5% contains five per cent flubendazole. 200mg (7oz) of Flubenol 5% is mixed with 100 litres (22gal) of water which is the equivalent of 10mg (0.35oz) of flubendazole per 100 litres (22gal) of tankwater. Its solubility has been the focus of many discussions. The easiest way is to mix the substance with warm water and then add it to the aquarium. The treatment should be repeated three times at weekly intervals. Flubenol 5% remains in the tank for three days after which time a partial

water change and an activated carbon filtration is carried out. The second treatment should be carried out a week later for three days and the final treatment seven days after that for another three days. Always carry out a partial water change before starting the repeat treatment. and ensure that the water is well aerated. Flubendazole is a slow-acting medication, as it blocks nutrients being absorbed into the gill flukes' intestines. So it is only possible to check if the treatment has been successful after the third application. It is not recommended that you carry out a flubendazole treatment too often as it may harm the fish. Of course this also applies to most other forms of treatment.

Naturally, there are a lot more medicines and diseases connected with discus. However, this concise book cannot cover all of them. Special publications on diseases and treatment are available.

Listed opposite are ten important rules which every discus lover should observe to prevent his or her fish succumbing to diseases.

Ten rules for healthy discus

1 Observe the fish carefully and look out for any symptoms of disease before purchasing new stock. Stay clear of darkly coloured, skinny fish, and those with deformed fins, holes in the head and white stringy faeces trailing behind.

2 Keep newly bought fish in a quarantine tank for at least six weeks.

3 Keep the quarantine tank completely separate from a breeding and show tank.

4 Never use any equipment from the quarantine tank in any other tank. Always wash and disinfect your hands and arms once you have finished work in the quarantine tank.

5 Never transfer plants from one tank to another without disinfecting them first.

6 Always keep your fish in well-maintained water and living conditions.

7 Always provide a balanced diet.

8 Only transfer completely healthy fish, which have undergone the appropriate quarantine period, into a breeding tank or show tank.

9 Always clean and disinfect the quarantine tank after each use.

10 Make sufficient time available to watch your fish. In this way you will soon notice if they are uncomfortable or show any signs of disease.

Buying the right discus

Discus are not cheap and your purchase is therefore a matter of trust. As a buyer you should observe a few ground rules which will reward you and save you a lot of trouble later on. Many years ago discus were bred with colours that were not genuine – a cobalt blue discus that was sold for a lot of money might later turn out to be an ordinary, not so colourful, turquoise blue discus. This happens very rarely nowadays as the quality of discus, especially in respect of colour, has improved considerably. Lighting plays an important role in a discus aquarium and it has a great effect on the colours. It is quite possible that a newly bought discus with average colours can develop into a magnificent colourful fish in a well-equipped and well-lit aquarium at home. The beautiful round bodyshape is also an important aspect of discus.

Discus with an elongated body have suffered somehow during their growth period and this stunted growth can never be corrected later in life. Always check that the eye of a discus is in perfect proportion to its body size. If it appears too large, it is an infallible sign of growth damage which can hardly ever be cured – even with the best care these discus will always suffer from stunted growth. When buying young discus always look out for fish with a tell-tale "knife-back". From the front these fish can be recognized by their small backs and their overall appearance is hollow. Such discus are often so badly damaged that only emergency treatment can save them. You should never buy these fish even if they are very cheap. Looking at a discus front-on from above, a healthy specimen should always be perfectly rounded. Always watch the fish you want to buy carefully for several minutes and check if they are swimming actively or hiding in a corner. Be wary of dark-coloured and shy discus. However, if the nine vertical stripes are dark, it is not necessarily an indication of illness. The faeces of healthy discus, depending on the type of food they are eating, should be a browny red or black. On no account should the faeces be white and stringy. Don't buy fish that are trailing along white, transparent jelly-like faeces, as they are infested with parasites. Holes in the head are also an indication of disease in discus. If the discus breathes very quickly and one of the gills lies tight shut, it could mean gill fluke infestation, though young discus also breathe quickly when they have just finished feeding. Another sign of gill fluke infestation is if the fish rub their gills against any of the fitments in the tank. Although gill fluke infestation is difficult to cure, it can be eradicated with a certain treatment routine.

Why not ask the shop owner to feed the discus so that you can see for yourself how much they are interested in food? Healthy discus devour their food greedily. However, discus should not consume too much food before they are transported or their faeces will contaminate the water.

Even young discus should have a near perfectly rounded body, which is an indication of good health.
Photo: Mori

Successful breeding

Provided you have the right pair, breeding discus is not too difficult. The perfect discus pair are hardly any work and worry for the breeder. But you will have to be very lucky to find the perfect breeding pair straight away – it is more likely that you will have to spend some time searching for the perfect match. One option is to buy young discus and wait until they are ready to breed after about one year. However, this does not guarantee that a male and female will pair up for breeding. Buying mature discus and keeping them in a suitably large tank is an alternative. Then it is possible that two discus will pair off and prepare for spawning. Another option is to buy a breeding pair from a reliable source. However, this is the most expensive choice as the seller is quite justified in demanding a high price for a good breeding pair. If you decide to rear young discus and hope to produce one or two breeding pairs, you should have at least 10 to 20 fish. Once they have found a partner, discus, like most other cichlids, are very loyal and they should not be separated once they

have successfully produced off-spring.

How do you sex discus? Unfortunately, discus do not have reliable external sexual characteristics, which makes it difficult to distinguish between males and females. The best time to determine the sex is of course during spawning. Although discus have a variety of characteristics which may give some indication of their sex, they are never 100 per cent reliable. Male discus often have larger heads than the females, especially those from the same brood. From the front the male's head looks much bigger and from the side it is rounder than that of the female. The heads of females appear more pointed from a side view. The fins are often used to determine the sex, as the dorsal and anal fins of the male are often longer

The body of the female of this pair of discus seen here on the right is covered in red spots, a characteristic which breeders try to intensify through selective breeding. Wild discus of this variety comes from the Tefé region of the Amazon. Photo: Mori

Male

Female

Distinguishing marks in the ventral fins to help determine the sex of discus.

than those of the female. The caudal fin of the male also appears to be wider than that of the female discus.

How to prepare for breeding discus

Many aquarists move their breeding pairs into special spawning tanks, which are very spartan, and often only contain an urn or a flowerpot on which the fish can lay their eggs. However, these spawning tanks have to be large enough to give the female sufficient space to hide from the male should he get too amorous. Changes in the water, a partial water exchange for example, can provide an incentive for the discus to spawn. This partial water exchange has a temporary effect on the water which transmits impulses to the breeding pair and leads to spawning. The daily change of water is one of the open secrets of discus farming in Southeast Asia. The first signs of discus preparing to spawn are obvious; both fish perform a courtship display during which they swim towards each other bowing and sometimes nudging each other on the side. Generally this courtship display is quite peaceful and you will notice a colour change at the rear of the discus' bodies, where the vertical stripes are now very pronounced and the fish take on an overall darker appearance. This is a sign that the fish are ready to spawn, especially when

they start cleaning. The spawning surface is thoroughly cleaned by mouth. These cleaning sessions can last for several hours during which the discus shake their bodies vigorously. This body shaking is also a sign that the fish are ready to spawn. Normally discus spawn during the early evening hours. The water temperature influences the incubation period so that the fry begin to hatch after 55 to 60 hours. This in turn means that hatching usually takes place during the early hours of the third day. As the parents care for and guard their brood throughout their growing period, it is important that they hatch in the morning so that when they are born in the wild a suitable place can be found to bed them. Immediately before spawning the discus intensify their cleaning activities, and the female is usually busier than the male. The female becomes more and more restless and practises spawning by swimming repeatedly to the spawning ground.

At first there are no eggs visible but soon the female begins to lay the first chain on the spawning surface. It is important now that the male follows the female to fertilize the eggs immediately and a continuous process of spawning and fertilizing begins, which some pairs perform in perfect rhythm and harmony.

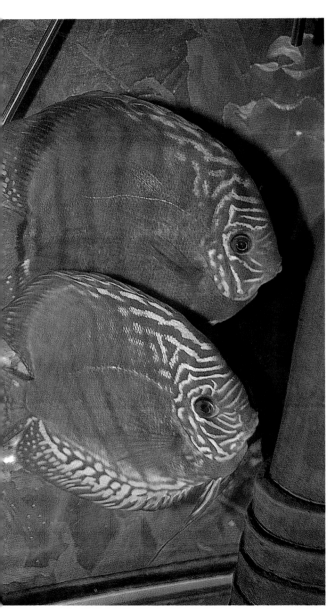

Spawning lasts approximately an hour during which time the female lays between 200 and 250 eggs on the breeding site. Immediately after spawning the parents begin looking after the eggs by fanning them gently with their pectoral fins, thus providing sufficient oxygen to prevent the eggs succumbing to a fungal disease. By fitting a small night-light above the tank you can ensure a better contact between the parents and the eggs and young fry.

Sadly, quite often discus eat all the eggs and so far the reason for this is unknown. An abnormality in the development of the eggs could be one reason for this unusual behaviour.

Discus spawning. The surface on which the eggs will be laid is thoroughly cleaned by the discus before spawning begins. This cleaning activity is a clear sign that the female is ready to spawn. A good pair of discus takes it in turns to guard the spawning site.

It is not unusual for some eggs to be attacked by fungus. Sometimes all the eggs will be destroyed; this is mostly caused by an imbalance in the water.

A devoted discus pair constantly fan the eggs to supply them with oxygen. Sometimes they also try to pick out the white eggs.
Photos: Mori

The parents seem to recognize that some-thing is wrong with the spawn and simply eat it, only to start spawning again after four to six days. If this happens, or the eggs are constantly attacked by fungus, then you must improve the quality of the water in the tank.

If, however, the eggs develop well, a nucleus becomes clearly visible after the second day

which is a sign that the egg is fertilized. The eggs with a dark nucleus have developed normally and on the third day movements in the eggs become clearly visible. The small discus fry hatch with their tails appearing first. The next development stage takes approximately 60 hours after which the fry can swim. The young discus begin to thrash around with their tails in an effort to free themselves from the spawning ground but an adhesive string attached to their heads keeps them secured. After approximately six days their development is complete and the young fry begin to swim away from the spawning surface. The parents try to prevent this happening by collecting their brood in their mouths. This can look quite dangerous to the inexperienced aquarist as it seems as if the parents are eating their young. But the parents only "chew" their young and then spit them out again onto the spawning surface. Finally, after some time, the parents are no longer able to collect all their young and so cannot prevent them from swimming around freely. It is now important that the fry swim to their parents. Dark-coloured discus begin to secrete a body "milk" on which the fry feed. The offspring are drawn to the dark body surface and immediately start

In this picture all the eggs have been attacked by fungus. In most cases these eggs will be eaten by the parents and just a few days later the female will begin spawning again.

feeding. It is very interesting to watch the young feeding as they greedily devour the slime from their parents' bodies. The parents constantly signal to their brood to feed and the young cling closer and closer to their parents' bodies. Very caring discus pairs take it in perfect turn to feed their brood. Unfortunately, adverse water conditions can lead to problems in the adult fish and their feeding of the young. Lack of mucus secretion is a well-known problem in Europe although in Southeast Asia it

The fry in this picture are being reared successfully. They are swimming close to their parents' bodies and feeding on the nutritious coat of slime produced for just this reason.

The young fish are feeding well on the body secretion and within a week they are ready to take newly hatched Artemia *brine shrimps. Photos: Mori*

problem. The parents' nutritious coat of slime is a vital food source for the fry during the first four to five days and if this is not available, the young cannot survive. The slime contains bacteria and algae which is the first food for the fry. It also provides carbohydrates, fats and proteins, which are important nutrients and strengthen their immune system. Five days after swimming independently, the young discus can be fed with *Artemia* shrimps, which every discus enthusiast can breed himself. The appropriate equipment can be bought in a specialist shop. Experts are divided on how long young discus should stay with their parents, but it is quite possible to leave them hardly ever occurs. This leads us to conclude that the condition of the water is the cause of any feeding

with their parents for up to four weeks so that they can enjoy the body slime as additional food. The young fish now grow more and more into the discus shape and also eat all kinds of fine fish food. During this phase you can introduce other types of fish food. After approximately four weeks the young discus are the size of a 10 pence piece and can now be separated from the parents.

Selective discus breeding

The vibrant coloured turquoise-blue discus or the luminous red discus sold now as selectively bred offspring did not exist 30 years ago. Some 40 years ago, when it became more common to export wild discus from Brazil to Europe, aquarists were just

The parents take it in turn to feed their young. If you have a pair which shares this task without fighting, then you are lucky to have found the perfect match. By twitching, the parents show their young where to swim.

If danger threatens, the fry quickly return to their parents. A whole swarm of young discus is your reward for the care that you have devoted to them. Photo: Mori

After two weeks the young fish already have the typical discus body shape.

A good discus pair share parental care and take it in turns to look after their young without fighting. The bond between parents and young is still very strong at this stage.

happy that these colourful fish were available at all and initially they were quite content with the appearance and colours of the discus that they received. However, as is always the case, mankind likes to change nature and even improve it and this he has done successfully with respect to the colours of the discus. In particular wild green discus with a soft green colouring, which distinguished them from other species, were chosen for breeding in order to intensify this solid

green coloration. Inbreeding and crossbreeding soon produced solid green discus – some with, others without, brown stripes.

Certain characteristics can be intensified and established through inbreeding, which means the crossing of siblings or off-spring with parents. However, as this is not a perfect solution in the long term, line breeding as well as inbreeding is necessary. In line breeding fish from two different breeding lines are crossed – the young then carry the hereditary characteristics of both breeding lines. By crossing the "best" of these offspring with the best offspring of another line, one gets closer to the ultimate goal of selective breeding.

Breeding discus in a tank which is stocked with aquatic plants is not impossible, but it is difficult. Other fish in the tank will regard the fry as food.

Wild green discus provide the basis for the brilliantly coloured turquoise fish which are bred world-wide today. Turquoise discus are available in all colour shades and are regarded as the colour standard.

Intensive selective breeding, mainly by Asian breeders, has made it possible to produce discus with interesting fixed strains that can be inherited. Bright colours are always at the forefront of the breeding effort. Photos: Mori

Of course it is essential to have the necessary space to carry out this type of line breeding consistently over many years and hardly any amateur breeder has such facilities. So it is that the discovery of a new colour variety, such as the pigeon-blood discus in 1990 in Thailand, is normally reserved for the large breeders of Southeast Asia. The discus is full of surprises and new colour variants will always be developed. Some change the world of discus breeding while others simply disappear from the scene.

Discus breeding in Asia

The economic significance of selective discus breeding was recognized as long as 20 years ago in Southeast Asia. Not only discus but many other ornamental fish are bred in vast

quantities there to satisfy the ever-growing worldwide demand. The main producers of discus are Thailand, Singapore, Hong Kong, Malaysia, the Philippines and Taiwan. The main purchasers of discus are the European nations, the USA and Japan.

Initially the quality of the fish was not an important criterion in Southeast Asia and breeding was randomly carried out simply to sell as many discus as possible. The reputation of Asian discus breeders was quickly ruined and German breeders especially profited from their demise as the quality of German-bred discus was amongst the highest. Since then several discus farms have been set up in Southeast Asia, many of which recognize the importance of quality – nowadays quality, as well as quantity, are the main criteria in discus breeding. Colour intensity and higher than average body proportions of the discus are most desirable

characteristics. With Japan establishing itself as one of the major markets for discus, breeders cater more and more for Japanese tastes, which results in a constant demand for more intense colours. Asian breeders are on a continuous hunt for new colour varieties and will go to extremes to create these.

Breeders in Asia soon realized that European-bred discus are of very high quality and therefore they bought

A magnificent brilliant turquoise blue discus bred in Asia. This breeding line originated in Germany. Photo: Aqualife Taiwan

In Southeast Asia the daily water change is always top of the agenda. Up to 90 per cent of the water is changed daily, which has a positive effect on the health of the fish and their readiness to spawn. Asian discus breeders know all sorts of tricks in order to produce young discus easily. Separating the parents from the fry to prevent them fighting over their offspring is just one of them.
Photos: Mori

vast stocks for breeding in order to establish large stocks of selectively bred discus. This increased the demand for Asian-bred discus and the growing numbers of discus farms made colour mutation inevit-

and it is easy to see why discus breeders are constantly searching for new varieties.

What is the difference between Southeast Asian and European breeding? The most significant difference is that discus breeding in Europe is primarily a hobby whereas in Southeast Asia it is a business. Even small breeders with only a few tanks, which are sometimes set up in their homes, depend on discus breeding for a living, as the tropical temperatures provide ideal conditions for it. In general there is no need to heat the aquarium which makes the whole operation cheaper and puts the Asian breeder at an advantage. Another advantage is that the water in Asia is of much higher quality than

able, which resulted in the ghost discus in Malaysia, the pigeon-blood discus in Thailand, and, later in Thailand, the snakeskin discus. All these new discus varieties could be certified as fixed (meaning that all characteristics will be inherited by future generations) and they appear today on every international price list.

New breeds or colour variants always fetch high prices on the market

does not mean that all Asian discus are cheap to buy; on the contrary new colour variants, for example, are often very expensive. Once a breeder has successfully bred a new colour variant and raised several broods displaying this new colour, he will create a new trade name and offer it for sale.

A significant difference to European discus breeding is the fact that professional Southeast Asian breeders rarely filter their water, but instead carry out a daily water change. As water is cheap

In Southeast Asia the pigeon-blood discus has been a real star over the last six years. This variety originated in Thailand and created much excitement on the international discus scene.

Breeding tanks in Asia are hardly ever fitted with filters or heaters as the daily water change in conjunction with the warm tropical climate means that they are unnecessary for discus care.
Photos: Mori

European tap water and a lot cheaper. It is also noticeable that the eggs of Southeast Asian-bred discus are not as susceptible to fungus as is so often the case in Europe. But cheap water, ideal water temperature and inexpensive locations are not the only advantages enjoyed by Asian breeders – lower living costs and low wages make even a medium-sized Asian operation competitive, and allow all Asian breeders to flood the market with cheap offers. However, this

*A "sun-red-turquoise" discus from Taiwan.
Photo: Mori*

and of good quality, up to 90 per cent of the water in the tanks is replaced. The fish respond well to these large-scale water changes – it promotes growth and can prevent many diseases. Despite this, breeders in many Asian countries like to use antibiotics as treatment for, or prevention of, diseases. This is the main reason why some pathogens are already resistant to many antibiotics which makes it quite difficult for aquarists in Europe to treat a number of diseases.

Asian discus lovers constantly invent new names for their fish just to keep the market buoyant. The discus pictured here is known as "Manacapuru red turquoise". Photo: Mori

A view of one of the most sophisticated breeding stations in Taiwan shows how they work with the appropriate filter technique. Even here water change is a daily routine.
Photos: Mori

Feeding is also very important to Asian breeders and they prefer to use live feed. While breeders in Hong Kong mainly feed red mosquito larvae, Thai breeders are still using Tubifex. In Malaysia red mosquito larvae and shrimps are the main food for discus, while Japanese discus breeders swear by so-called "hamburgers" made of beefheart and other ingredients, which are frozen and sold in aquatic shops.

The discus market in Southeast Asia has not yet peaked and new breeding centres open up everywhere to sell their fish. This will eventually lead to the normal, simply bred turquoise variant and the red-turquoise discus becoming much more widely available to members of the public at surprisingly low prices. However, the quality of these mass-produced fish may then be compromised.

We, as amateur breeders, should try to retain the beautiful shape of the discus and take pleasure in the quiet enjoyment of their majestic swimming behaviour and devoted care of their offspring. Mass breeding on a commercial scale should never be at the forefront of a hobby; it would spoil the fun of the pastime and make this type of fishkeeping become a routine just like work.

The very light "ghost discus" was first bred in Penang in Malaysia. Photo: Mori

The magnificent colours of discus

When the discus boom began in Europe in the 1960s, many wild discus were available to the hobby aquarist. Brown and green were the most common colours as nature had intended. Enthusiastic breeders soon concentrated their efforts on how to change and intensify the colours of the offspring. But how can you change the colour of a fish? Selective breeding is the simplest option, which enables the breeder to keep large stocks of discus and to crossbreed those fish with the most intense colours. The young of this brood with the most interesting colours are then selected for further breeding. Inbreeding can also produce good results, where, for example, siblings or parents and offspring are crossbred to strengthen colour characteristics. It is thanks to the persistence and imagination of breeders that more vibrant and intensely coloured discus are available on the market. At first wild green discus were bred gradually to pro-

A young brilliant turquoise discus such as is bred today in large quantities in Southeast Asia.
Photo: Mori

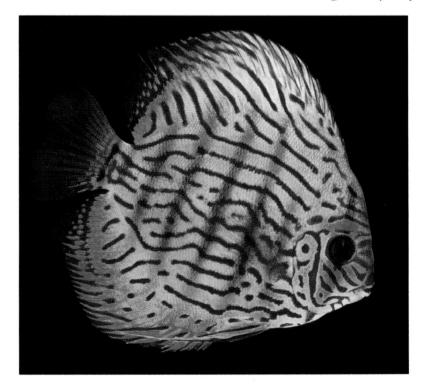

duce more intense turquoise fish. These turquoise-coloured discus soon become the object of everyone's desire.

Numerous colour descriptions have been created worldwide for discus and many of the names, especially those created in Southeast Asia, are no longer comprehensible. The name "turquoise discus" was probably the first artificial name given to a young discus which no longer displayed the same colours as the wild stock.

It made sense to breed turquoise discus which had developed from wild stock. The colour of the discus had to become more and more intense. The turquoise discus still showed traces of the brown base colour and so breeders endeavoured to eliminate this coloration. Turquoise discus were much in demand and selective breeding produced stocks with a more intense colour; eventually discus were bred in beautiful turquoise colours and a new name soon appeared on the breeders' lists, Brilliant Turquoise. Brilliant turquoise means a colour improvement on the turquoise discus. However, the difference between the turquoise and brilliant turquoise discus is vague and difficult to define.

The name turquoise discus was soon introduced worldwide and fish were traded at high prices. This global name for all turquoise coloured discus soon achieved world fame and discus fans worldwide were keen to buy these pretty fish. The whole body of the discus is covered with turquoise stripes with only a trace of brownish stripes appearing on the underside of the fish. In general more than 50 per cent of the discus' colour is made up of these turquoise stripes. The brown-red ground colour was gradually reduced, and in some brightly coloured discus

To breed a high-body and high-finned discus is one of the most desirable goals in Southeast Asia. The high-fin shape of this brilliant turquoise discus is already quite noticeable. Photo: Mori

Magnificent colours

The red-brown stripes of this pair of brilliant turquoise have faded and they can almost be described as solid blues.

The high dorsal fin of this turquoise discus is already well developed. The high fins will be beautifully formed by the time the discus is two years old. Photos: Mori

very few single stripes or areas were visible. Depending on the colour type, the turquoise can look so intense that they could almost be called solid turquoise discus. However, the overall appearance of the discus also depends on the lighting in the aquarium and you the turquoise ground colour is so dominant that it simply complements the turquoise stripes.

The colour of brilliant turquoise discus is particularly intense around the head and back. Subsequently they were sold under the name brilliant turquoise. They showed even fewer signs of the brown ground colour as breeders succeeded in reducing this colour to such an extent that only

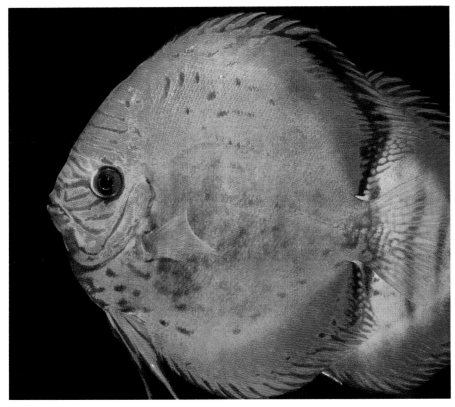

The colour of this discus is a strong blue, which also justifies its name "cobalt blue".
Photo: Mori

can achieve completely different results once the correct lighting has been installed. The mood of the discus can also affect their appearance, and they certainly will not display vibrant colours if they feel unwell.

The colour of a healthy brilliant turquoise discus should be vibrant and glowing turquoise. To the admirer the fish should seem to have a metallic glow. If the colour is flat rather than glowing, then the discus should not be sold as a brilliant turquoise. While the turquoise discus is still popular on the market, it has by now been demoted to the status of a mass-produced fish. Nowadays it is possible to breed and sell vast quantities of this discus. They have become the beginners' discus, but breeders have a responsibility to breed only from clean-coloured

71

Turquoise discus with vibrant brown stripes known in Asia as "Manacapuru red turquoise". The name is derived from a similar wild species found in the Rio Manacapuru. It is purely a trade name though.
Photo: Mori

species and they should not succumb to commercial demand and use any turquoise coloured discus for breeding. This is the only way to guarantee a certain standard in the quality of discus. Turquoise discus are very robust and can be recommended to every beginner aquarist.

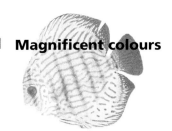

Red-turquoise discus

Red has always been a desirable colour in any ornamental fish. It is easy to see why, as red dots are very conspicuous in an aquarium. However, this colour simply does not exist in the wild. Although some wild discus species have a red ventral fin or show traces of red on the edges of their fins, the colour of their body is never really red. Some brown wild discus species have red spots or reddish body parts, but they do not qualify to be called a red discus. The red discus as such did not exist, but discus breeders and buyers alike longed for such a coloured fish. This explains why so many owners tend to see more red in their own fish than any critical observer.

The colour can also be dependent on the type of food and lighting available. It is quite possible either to make the colour visible or optically to enhance it by installing special lighting. But the pretty colour does not show on a photograph taken with flash. Certain types of food can also enhance the colour and even produce the colour in a discus. Any feed containing carotene will naturally improve all shades of red in any fish. It is also quite harmless to use these foods provided they are made of natural dietary substances. Of course no respectable breeder

Another variety of the so-called "Manacapuru red turquoise". These fish are currently very popular – especially those with a vibrant red-brown ground colour.
Photo: Mori

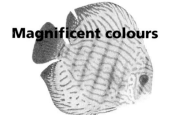

should ever resort to using artificial hormones in an attempt to achieve the right colouring.

The search for red discus made the wild brown discus unpopular and they were neglected for many years. Only in recent years has their popularity increased again and these beautiful species are a real asset to the discus aquarium. While turquoise discus were conquering the aquarists' world, all other discus varieties had to take a back seat. However, eventually it was discovered that even some turquoise discus have strong red-brownish stripes. By crossing red-brown discus with the turquoise variety, it became possible to breed well-balanced turquoise-coloured discus. Slowly more and more breeders became interested in red-turquoise colours and concentrated their efforts on breeding discus with this particular colour strain. German breeders especially favoured the red-turquoise discus and subsequently German-bred species enjoyed international acclaim. Suddenly you could buy a typical German red-turquoise discus. Compared to an ordinary turquoise discus, the red-turquoise shows predominantly red-brown lines interspersed with strong turquoise stripes. The red-turquoise colouring is even more intense around the fins. Depending on the

breeding line, it was possible to produce varieties with broad or fine reddish-brown stripes. It was these fine red-brown stripes appearing on strongly turquoise-coloured discus that made the red-turquoise discus highly desirable.

Asian breeders very quickly acquired large quantities of German-bred red-turquoise discus and they succeeded in concentrating their breeding to produce stunningly beautiful fish with tiny red spots and thin stripes.

No other discus variety shows a broader colour spectrum than the red-turquoise discus, which makes it very difficult to place red-turquoise discus in this colour group. If the stripes are not predominantly red, they should be categorized as ordinary turquoise discus, a decision no breeder likes to make.

A group of adult red-turquoise discus in a tank with a sand substrate and bright green plants provides a beautiful show for any discus fancier and hardly any other variety can compete with the beauty of red-turquoise discus.

Red discus
Bright red discus do not exist in the wild. For many years aquarists simply accepted the fact that this variety was not available. However, as soon as the

Breeders in Hong Kong produce crossbreeds from green Tefé discus. Their bodies are covered in red spots and they are called "red diamond" discus. However, it is very difficult to reproduce large numbers of these discus with such intense spots.
Photo: Mori

brown discus increased in popularity again, strongly red-brown wild species quickly appeared on the market. They were introduced as Alenquer discus and suddenly breeders worldwide couldn't get enough of this variety.

Steel blue and with a massive circular body, this cobalt blue discus swims towards the camera. Such huge discus are always admired by fanciers at shows, but a lot of effort is required to produce such a perfect specimen. Photo: Mori

The spell was finally broken when breeders in Thailand bred the pigeon-blood variety with interesting red colourings.

By crossing the Alenquer and pigeon-blood discus they created a new discus variety with an intensive red ground colour. A combination of

circumstances now made it possible to breed almost solid red-coloured discus. It should also be noted that this red colour is hereditary and cannot be achieved through feeding. These red discus were sold in Thailand as "Marlboro red" and it is quite remarkable that their whole body is red while the head is a yellow-brownish colour. The development of this colour strain is happening so quickly that amazing pictures of new red discus appear each year. Through continual breeding of all discus varieties, Asian breeders are constantly searching for new colour varieties. Sadly, they do not concentrate long enough on a specific colour in order to set it sufficiently, but instead carry on their breeding programme, as with the Marlboro discus for example to create a red snakeskin discus. The speed in breeding for new colour variants is rapidly increasing, as is the confusion over the names and appearance of these fish – a development which is not a good one.

Cobalt blue discus

Breeders may have succeeded in producing turquoise discus but they were not happy until the last brown stripes could be eliminated from the body. Their aim was to breed solid green or blue discus and we now know that it is possible. Today there are numerous discus with cobalt blue bodies, whose beauty cannot be surpassed. But how was it possible to retain the solid blue body of the discus? Selective breeding, inbreeding and consistent line breeding made it possible to remove the last vestige of brown stripes. This new discus generation displayed a shining metallic body after only two months and later the colour became so intense that all traces of brown stripes had disappeared. The brown stripes were still visible during their adolescence, though it could not

This picture shows a high-finned brilliant turquoise discus bred in Hong Kong. The colour is somewhat pale but the body shape is very tall. Photo: Mori

In 1990 a new type of discus, "pigeon-blood" conquered the world. Pigeon-blood discus are undemanding in their keep, which makes them very popular.
Photo: Mori

always be guaranteed that every fish from the same brood would have the same colour characteristics. Breeders suffered several set-backs and some aquarists must have felt cheated, having acquired ten young solid blue discus, only to discover that, once fully grown, only very few retained their original colouring. This was certainly not deception on the breeders' part as it is incredibly difficult to fix this characteristic through breeding. Even parents with perfectly coloured bodies can produce offspring with stripes. All

solid-coloured discus have perfect body markings, but brown lines were always visible around the head. This was the norm for many years until breeders in Hong Kong produced solid coloured discus without any stripes at all. These so-called "blue diamond" discus were the first discus with a solid-coloured head and as such were very rare and expensive. A discus with an almost solid silver coloured body was bred in Southeast Asia and appropriately named "ghost discus". These strains were then crossbred with other colour varieties

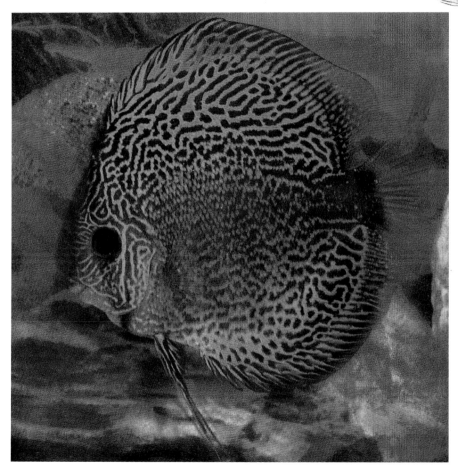

Discus lovers are constantly surprised by new shapes and colours. Only recently so-called King Cobra discus appeared on the Southeast Asian market. Similar discus were also sold as "snakeskin" discus. Their name is derived from their metallic shiny scales, which look like a snake's skin.
Photo: Mori

to create new characteristics. Solid blue discus are still highly desirable and are considered to be one of the highlights of a discus aquarium.

Because of their unique behaviour and varied appearance, aquarists around the world are enthusiastic about discus. This is also the reason why the discus will remain the uncrowned king of the freshwater aquarium. Once you have read this book, I hope that you will agree with me that discus are the most fascinating fish in any aquarium.

For further information
about the full Interpet range of
aquatic and pet titles, please
write to:
Interpet Publishing,
Vincent Lane,
Dorking,
Surrey,
RH4 3YX